Mr. Awkward
and other comics

ALSO BY THE AUTHOR

*The Dirty Parts of the Bible: A Novel*

*The Book of Craw: A Hobo's Testament*

# Mr. Awkward

### and other comics

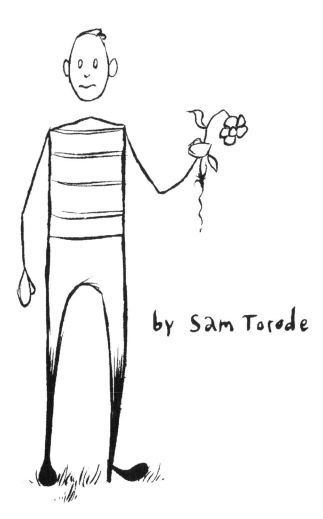

by Sam Torode

Comprised of works created from 1995–2006.



Printed in the USA.

# CONTENTS

# I.
# The Art of Being Awkward

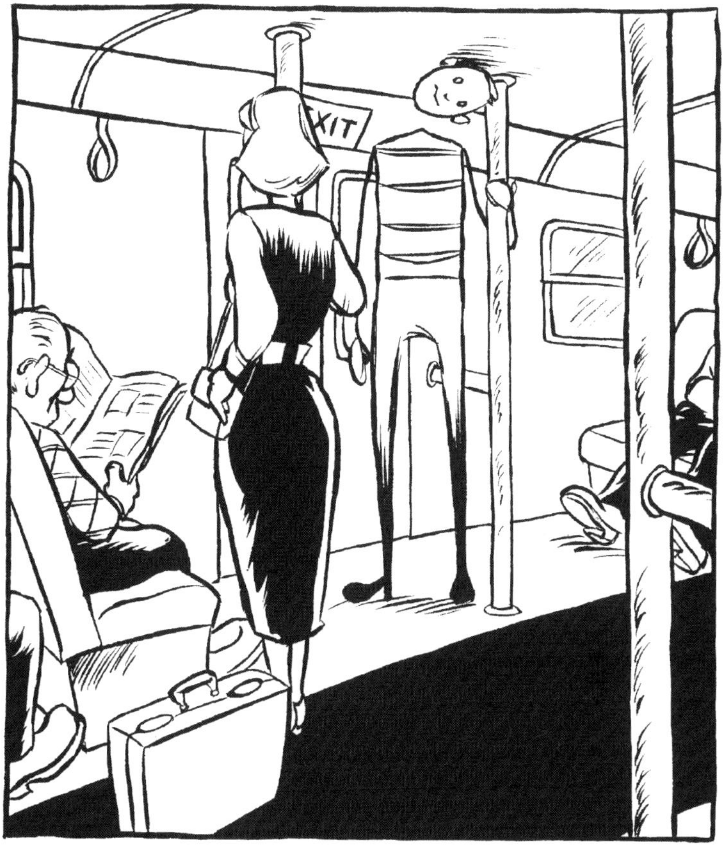
EXIT

Mr. Awkward is riding the subway.
Can you spot Mr. Awkward?

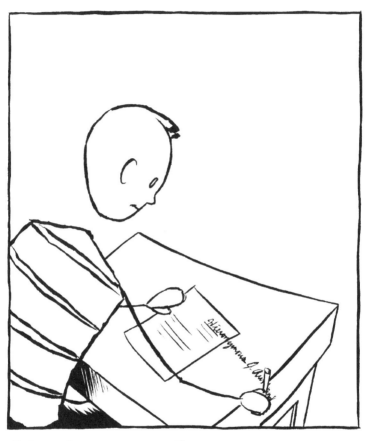

Mr. Awkward's name never
fits in the provided space

an awkward silence

Mr. Awkward is
awkward at parties

Amusement parks aren't
so amusing for Mr. Awkward

Sprorts do not agree
with Mr. Awkward

an awkward child

Mr. Awkward doesn't
"fit in" at school

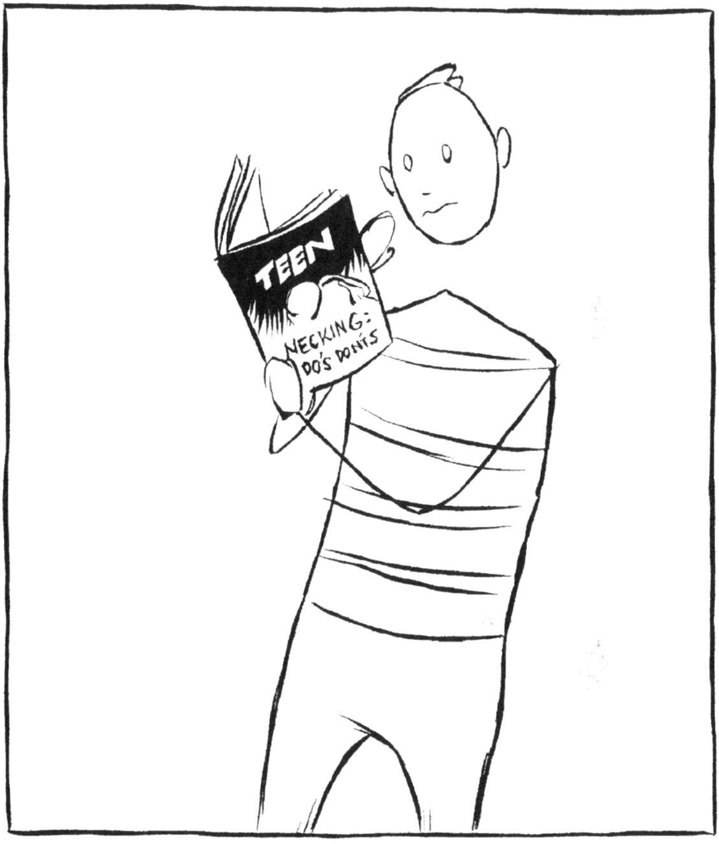
TEEN
NECKING:
DO'S DON'TS

the awkward age

Abraham Lincoln:
the awkward president

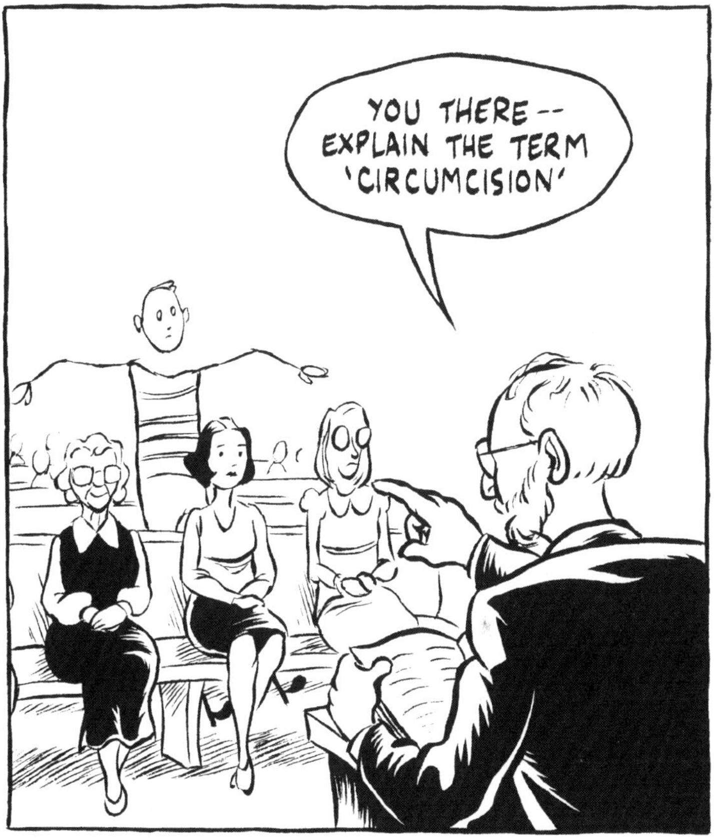
YOU THERE-- EXPLAIN THE TERM 'CIRCUMCISION'

in Sunday school

Economy cars are taxing
for Mr. Awkward

Suits don't suit
Mr. Awkward

the art of
being awkward

Nighty night,
Mr. Awkward

# II.
# The Ballad
# of Young Billy

# monkey bars

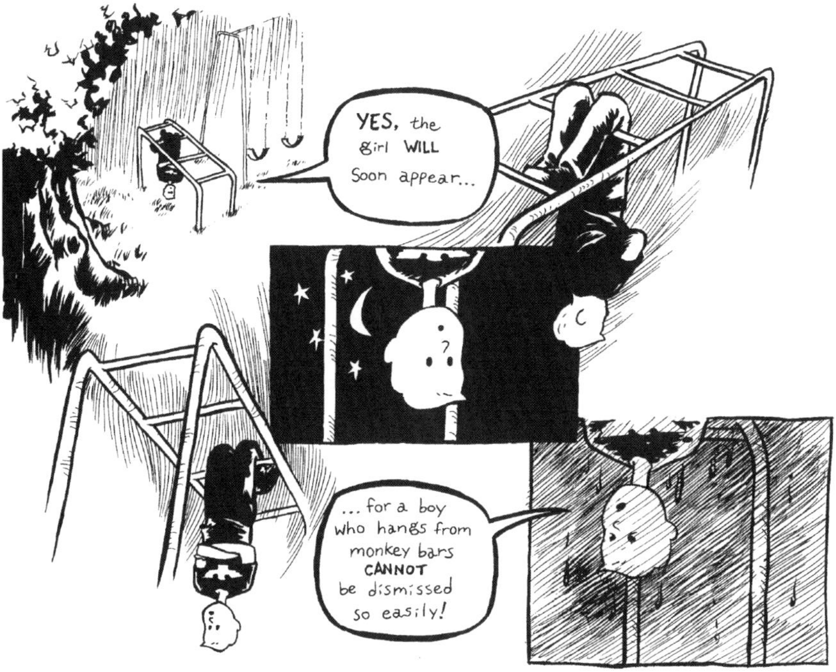
YES, the girl WILL Soon appear...
...for a boy who hangs from monkey bars CANNOT be dismissed so easily!

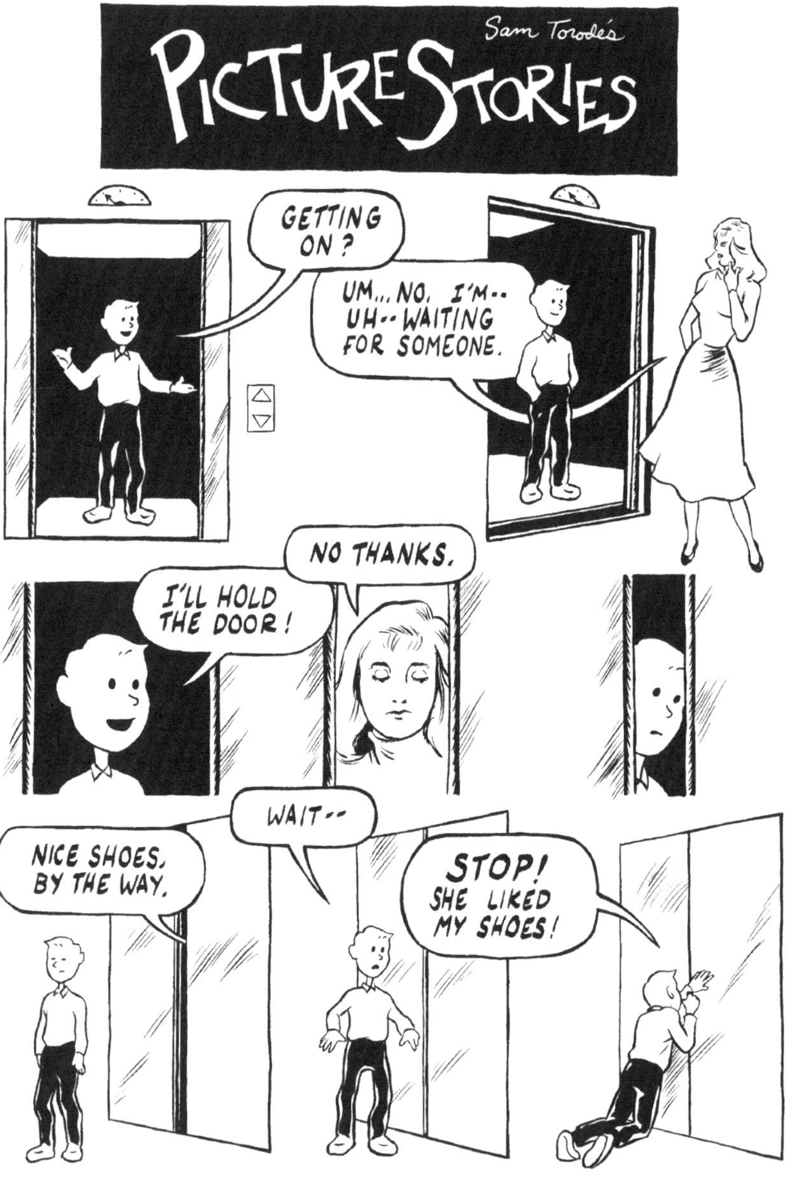
Sam Torode's
PICTURE STORIES
GETTING ON?
UM... NO. I'M-- UH--WAITING FOR SOMEONE.
I'LL HOLD THE DOOR!
NO THANKS.
NICE SHOES. BY THE WAY.
WAIT--
STOP! SHE LIKED MY SHOES!

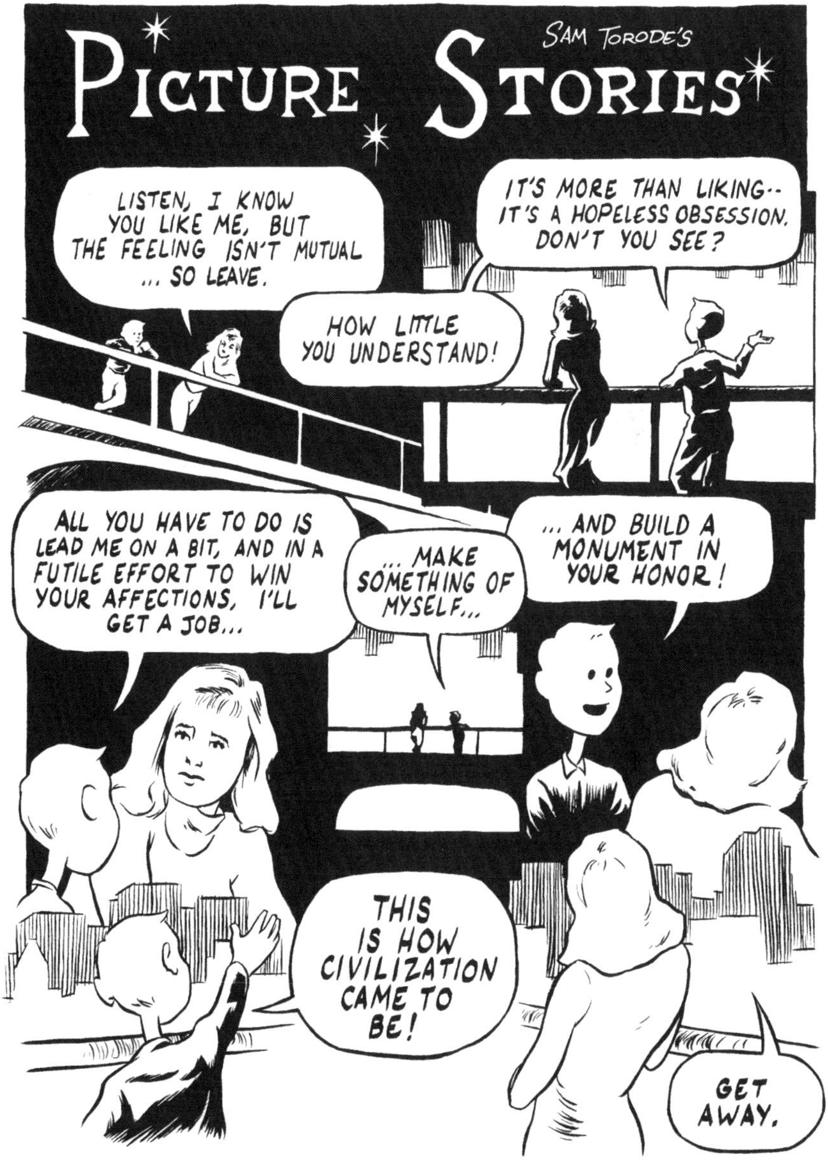
SAM TORODE'S
PICTURE STORIES
LISTEN, I KNOW YOU LIKE ME, BUT THE FEELING ISN'T MUTUAL ... SO LEAVE.
HOW LITTLE YOU UNDERSTAND!
IT'S MORE THAN LIKING.. IT'S A HOPELESS OBSESSION. DON'T YOU SEE?
ALL YOU HAVE TO DO IS LEAD ME ON A BIT, AND IN A FUTILE EFFORT TO WIN YOUR AFFECTIONS, I'LL GET A JOB...
... MAKE SOMETHING OF MYSELF...
... AND BUILD A MONUMENT IN YOUR HONOR!
THIS IS HOW CIVILIZATION CAME TO BE!
GET AWAY.

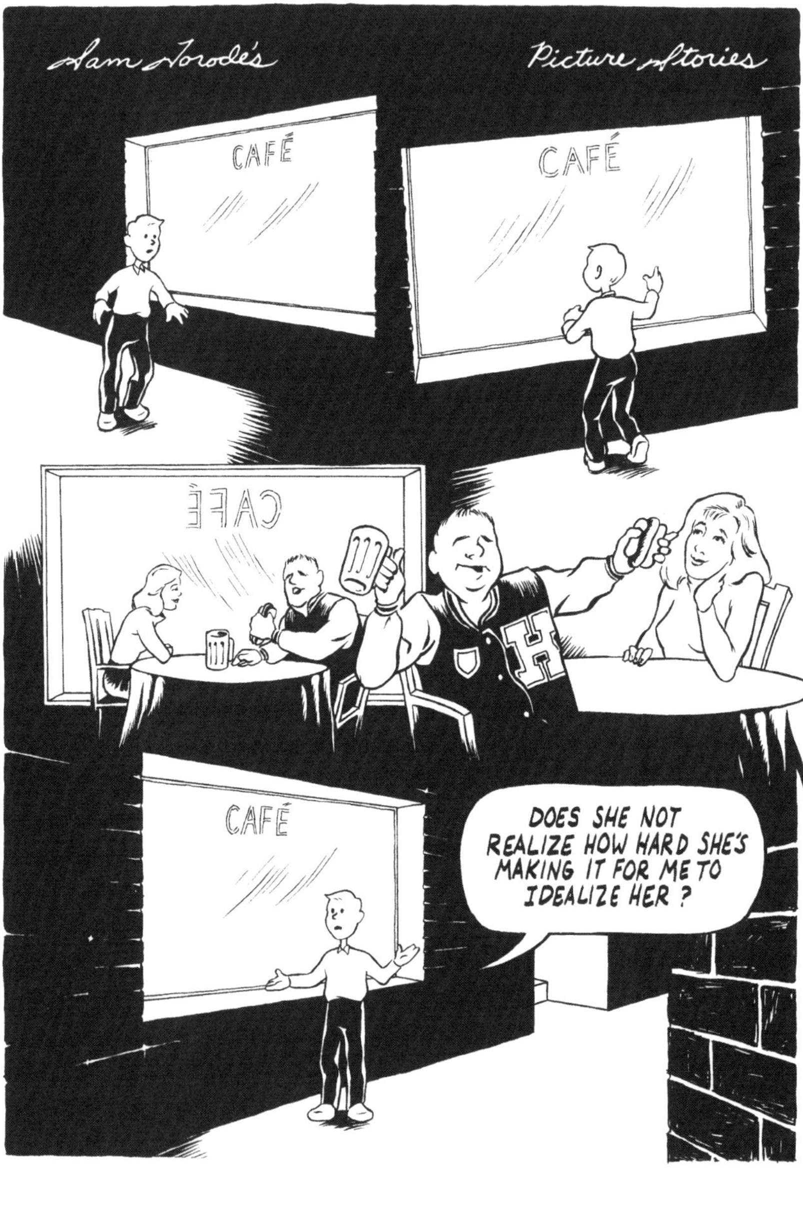
Sam Torode's
Picture Stories
CAFÉ
CAFÉ
CAFÉ
CAFÉ
DOES SHE NOT REALIZE HOW HARD SHE'S MAKING IT FOR ME TO IDEALIZE HER ?

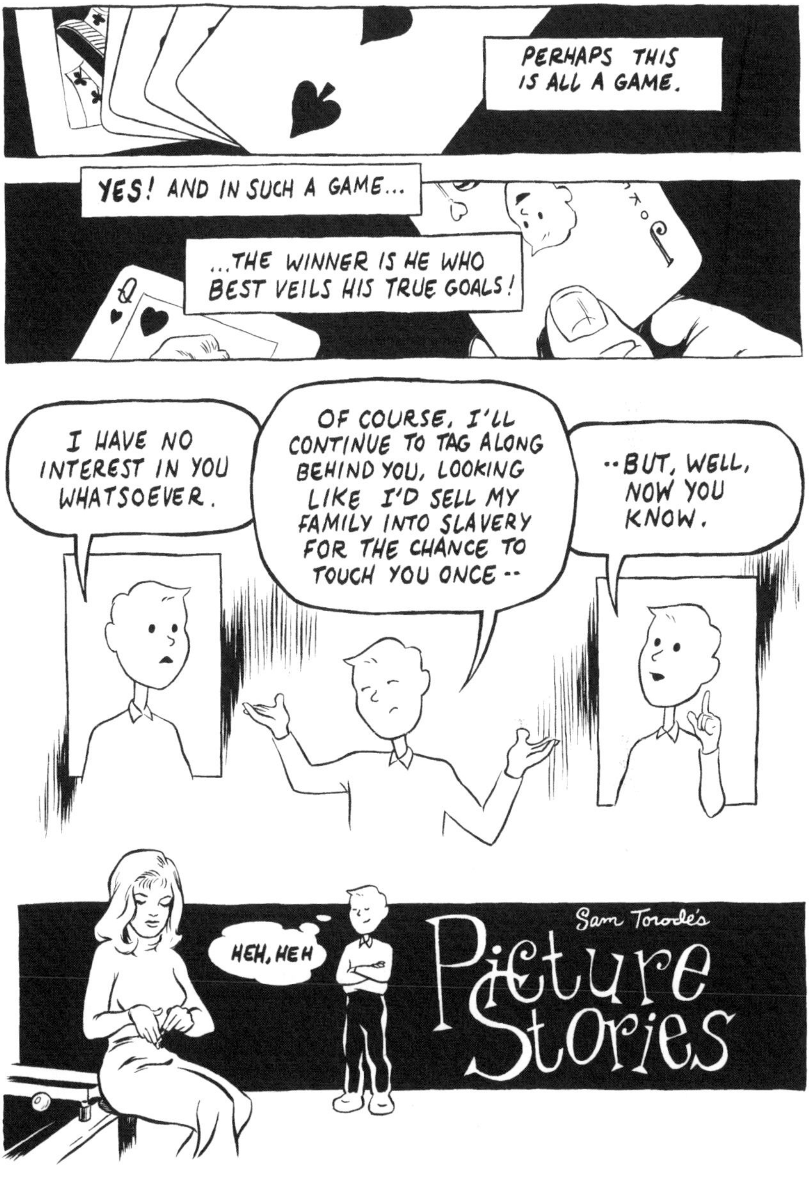
PERHAPS THIS IS ALL A GAME.
YES! AND IN SUCH A GAME...
...THE WINNER IS HE WHO BEST VEILS HIS TRUE GOALS!
I HAVE NO INTEREST IN YOU WHATSOEVER.
OF COURSE, I'LL CONTINUE TO TAG ALONG BEHIND YOU, LOOKING LIKE I'D SELL MY FAMILY INTO SLAVERY FOR THE CHANCE TO TOUCH YOU ONCE --
-- BUT, WELL, NOW YOU KNOW.
HEH, HEH
Sam Torode's
Picture Stories

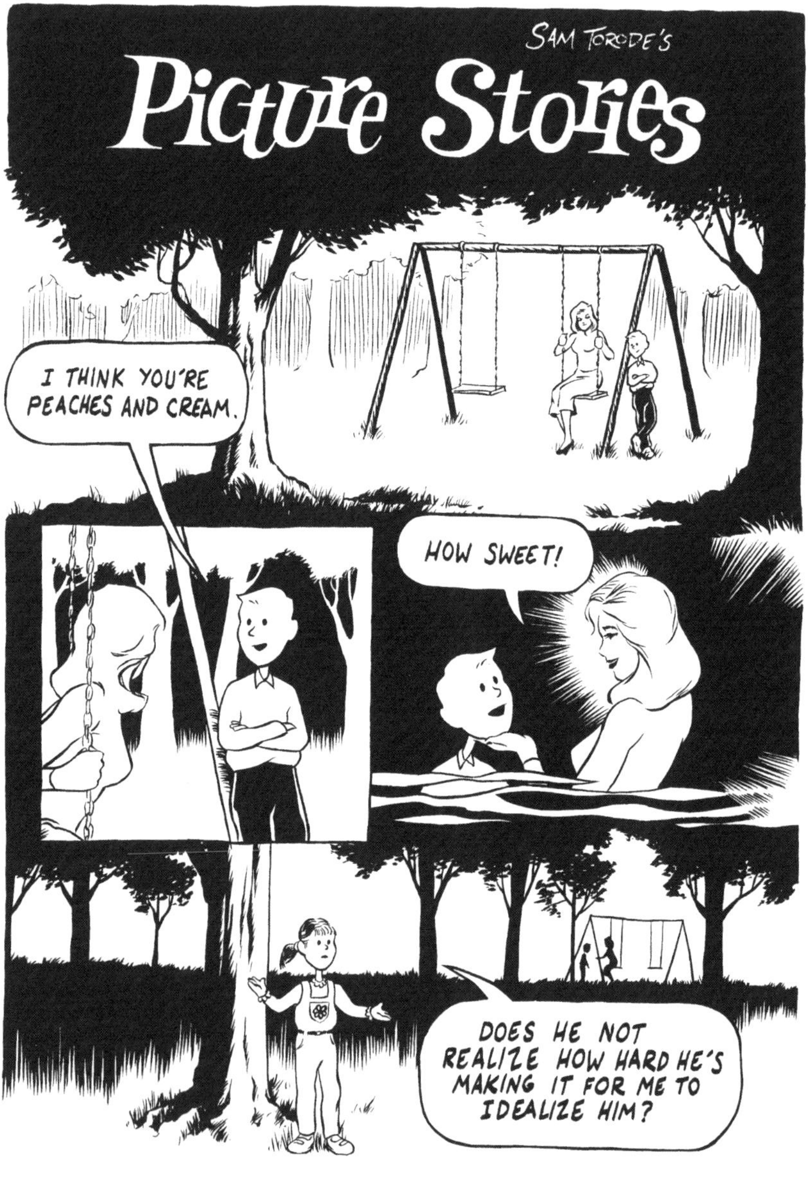
SAM TORODE'S
Picture Stories
I THINK YOU'RE PEACHES AND CREAM.
HOW SWEET!
DOES HE NOT REALIZE HOW HARD HE'S MAKING IT FOR ME TO IDEALIZE HIM?

# Farmer Billy

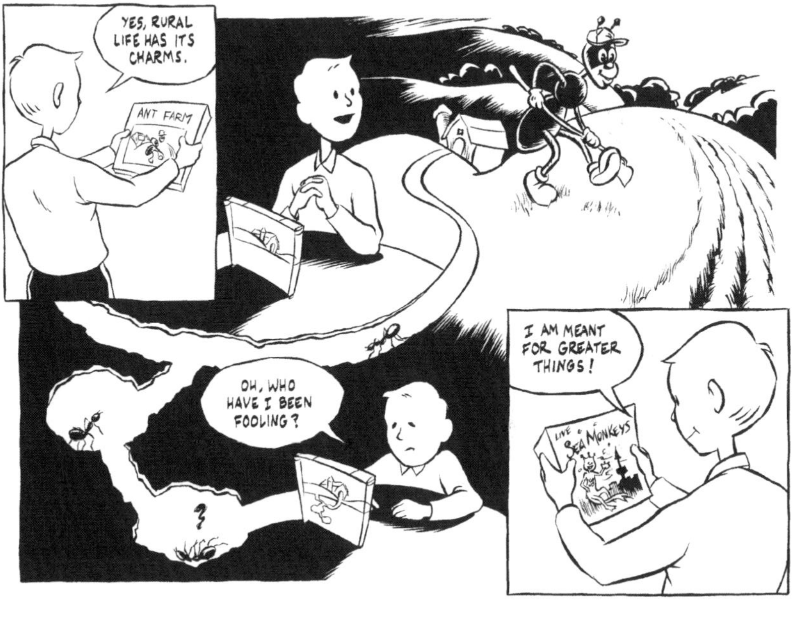
YES, RURAL LIFE HAS ITS CHARMS.
ANT FARM
OH, WHO HAVE I BEEN FOOLING?
I AM MEANT FOR GREATER THINGS!
LIVE SEA MONKEYS

# Valentine's Day

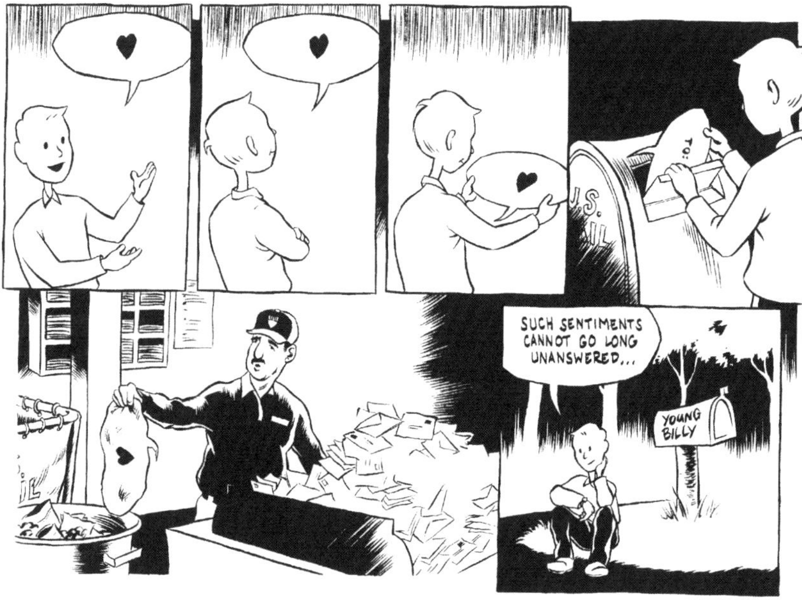

TO:
U.S. MAIL
SUCH SENTIMENTS CANNOT GO LONG UNANSWERED...
YOUNG BILLY

# III.
# The Futility
# of It All

# string theory

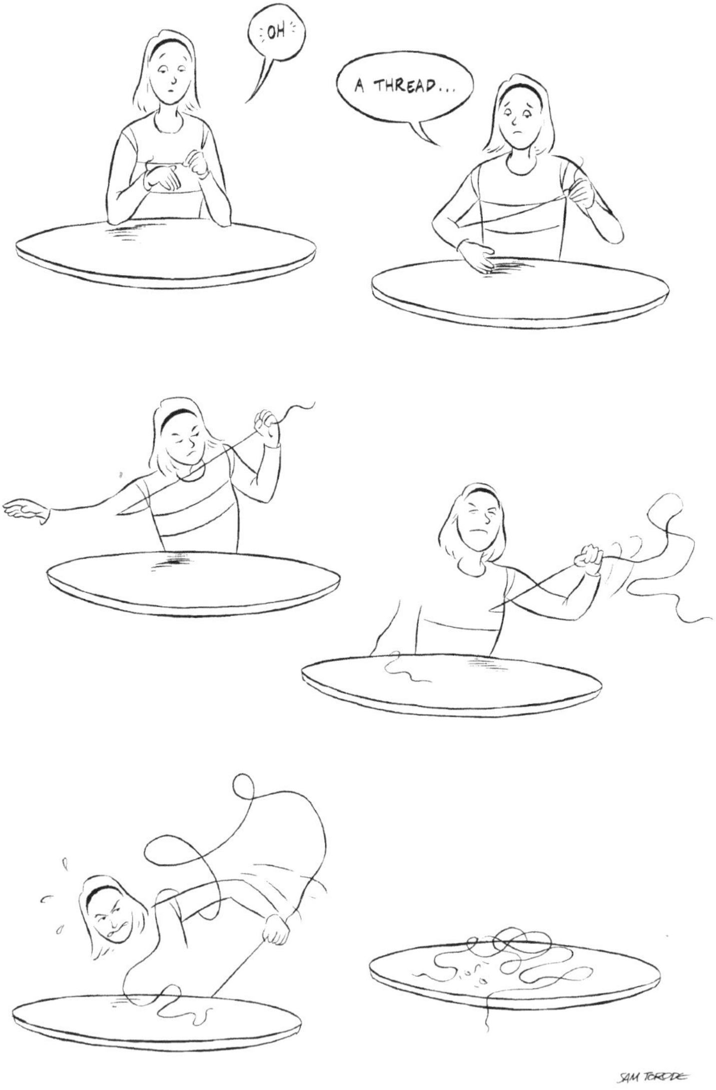
OH
A THREAD...
SAM TORODE

# Optimist vs. Pessimist

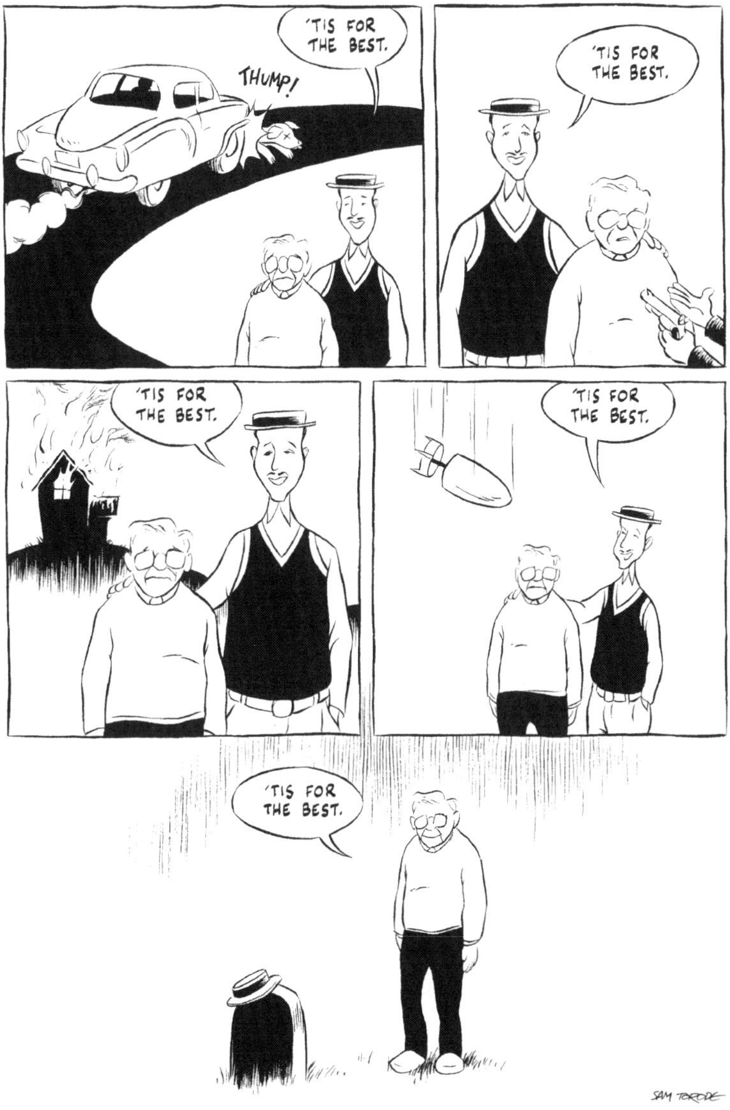
'TIS FOR THE BEST.
THUMP!
'TIS FOR THE BEST.
'TIS FOR THE BEST.
'TIS FOR THE BEST.
'TIS FOR THE BEST.
SAM TORODE

# The story of David

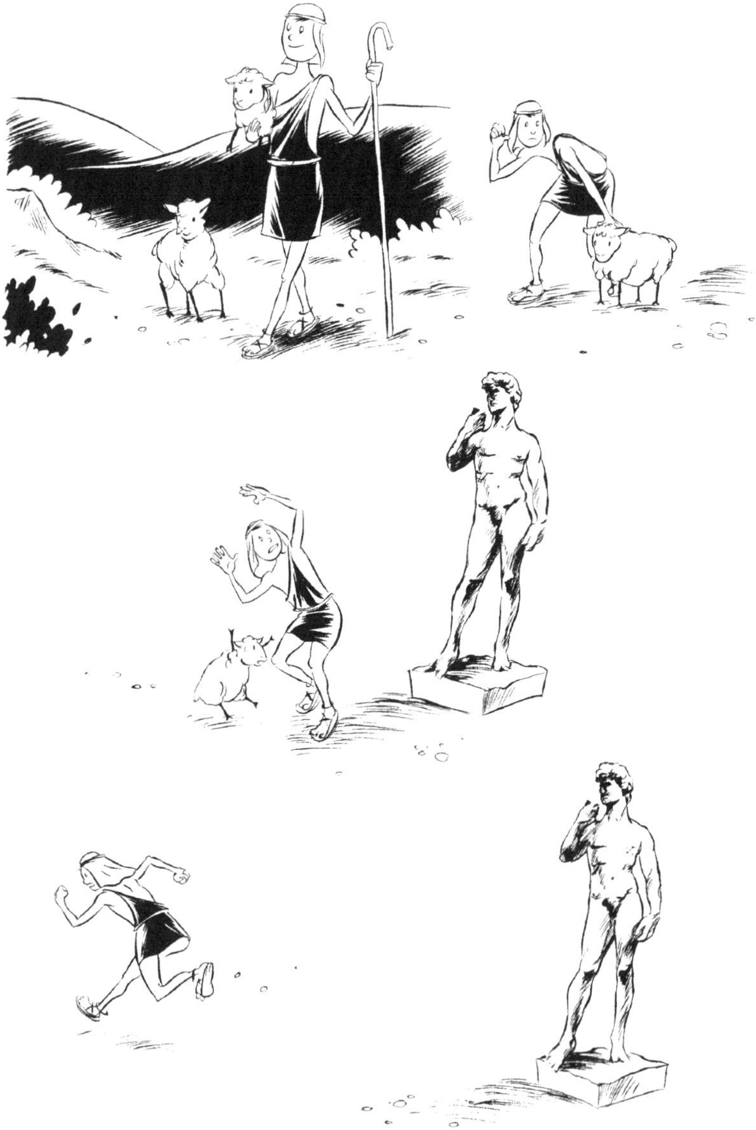

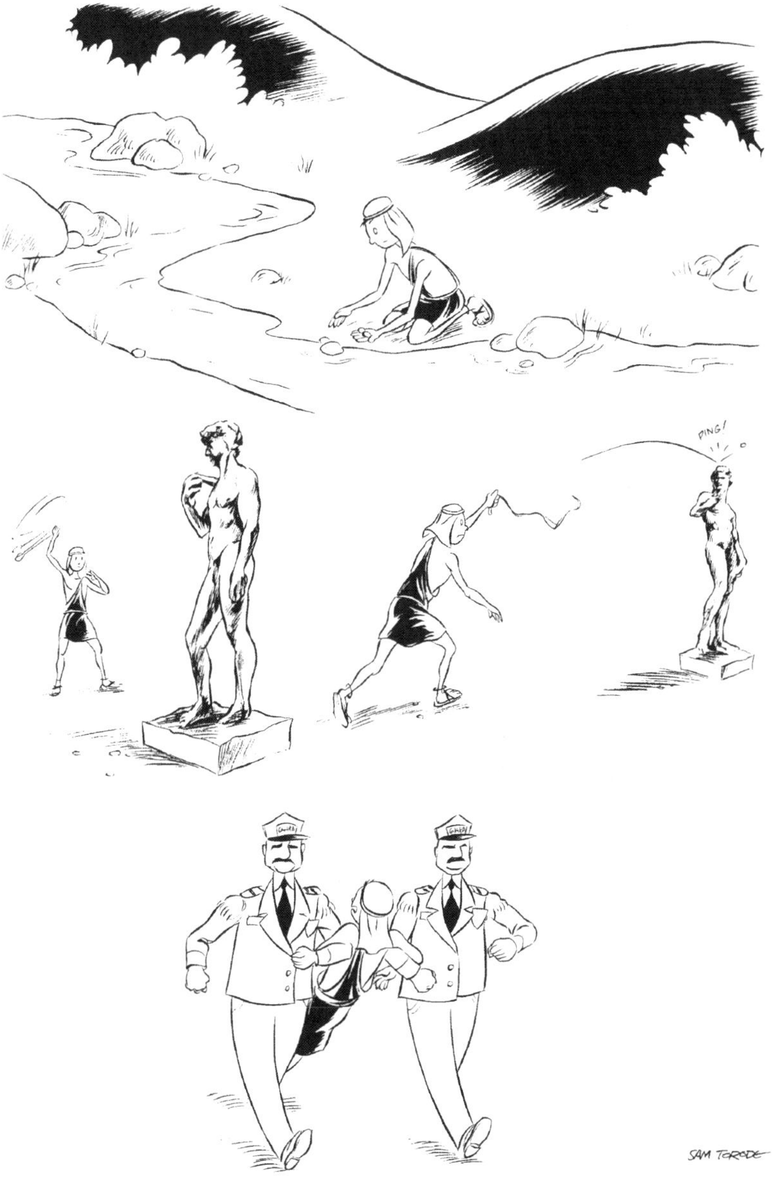
PING!
SAM TORODE

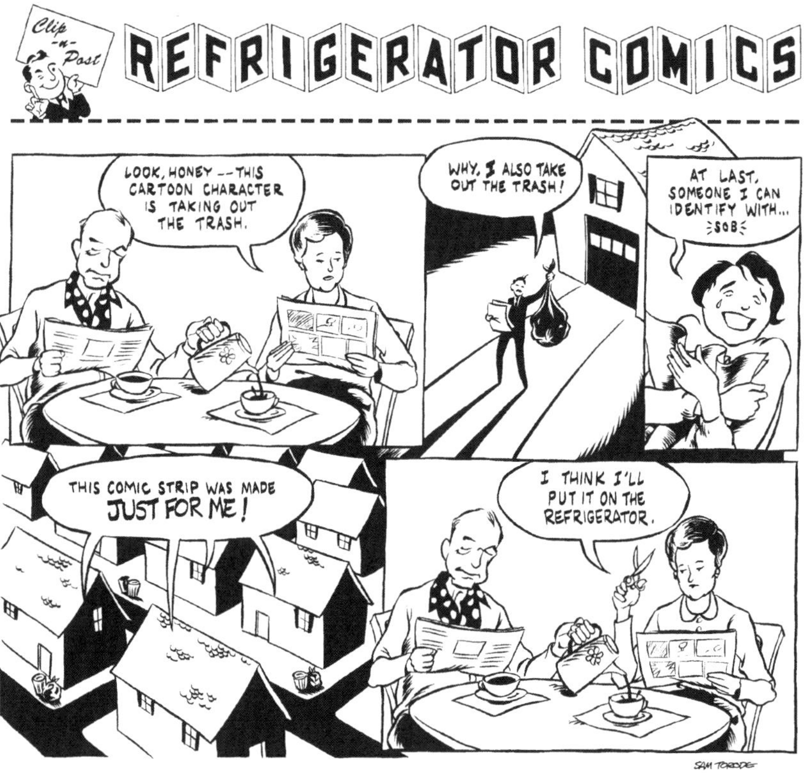
Clip -n- Post
REFRIGERATOR COMICS
LOOK, HONEY --THIS CARTOON CHARACTER IS TAKING OUT THE TRASH.
WHY, I ALSO TAKE OUT THE TRASH!
AT LAST, SOMEONE I CAN IDENTIFY WITH... SOB
THIS COMIC STRIP WAS MADE JUST FOR ME!
I THINK I'LL PUT IT ON THE REFRIGERATOR.
SAM TORODE

## Saturday at the Lawn & Garden

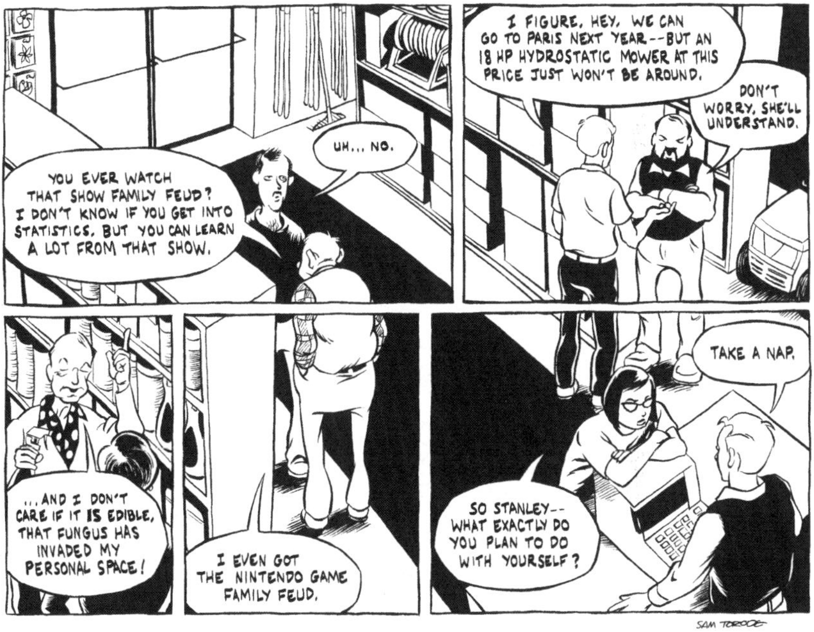
YOU EVER WATCH THAT SHOW FAMILY FEUD? I DON'T KNOW IF YOU GET INTO STATISTICS, BUT YOU CAN LEARN A LOT FROM THAT SHOW.
UH... NO.
I FIGURE, HEY, WE CAN GO TO PARIS NEXT YEAR--BUT AN 18 HP HYDROSTATIC MOWER AT THIS PRICE JUST WON'T BE AROUND.
DON'T WORRY, SHE'LL UNDERSTAND.
...AND I DON'T CARE IF IT IS EDIBLE, THAT FUNGUS HAS INVADED MY PERSONAL SPACE!
I EVEN GOT THE NINTENDO GAME FAMILY FEUD.
SO STANLEY-- WHAT EXACTLY DO YOU PLAN TO DO WITH YOURSELF?
TAKE A NAP.
SAM TOROODE

The Dali Llama

This is George.
He was a depraved
little monkey
and very sinful.

Calvinist bedtime stories

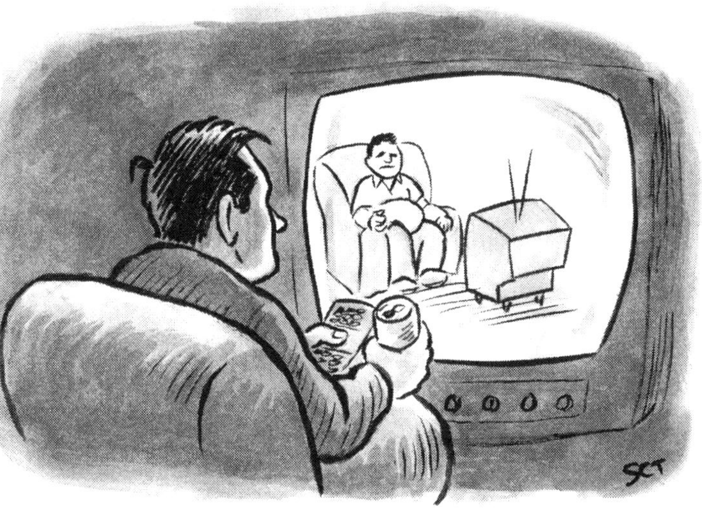
SCT

True reality TV

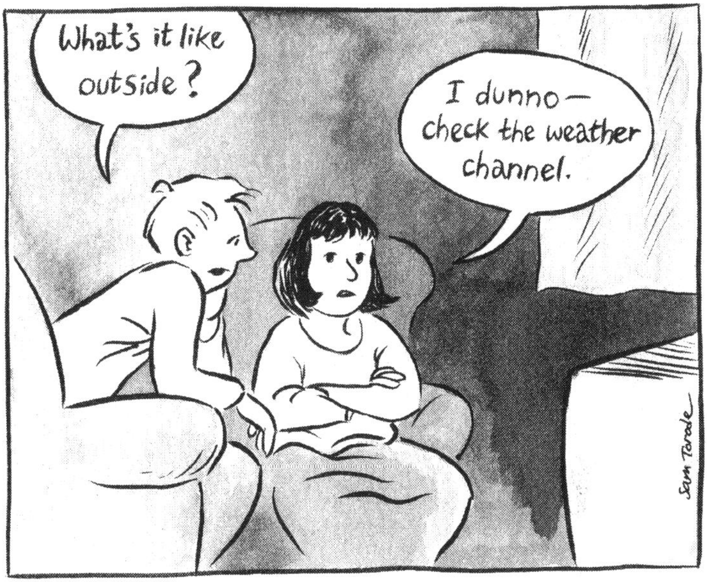
What's it like outside?
I dunno— check the weather channel.
Sam Torode

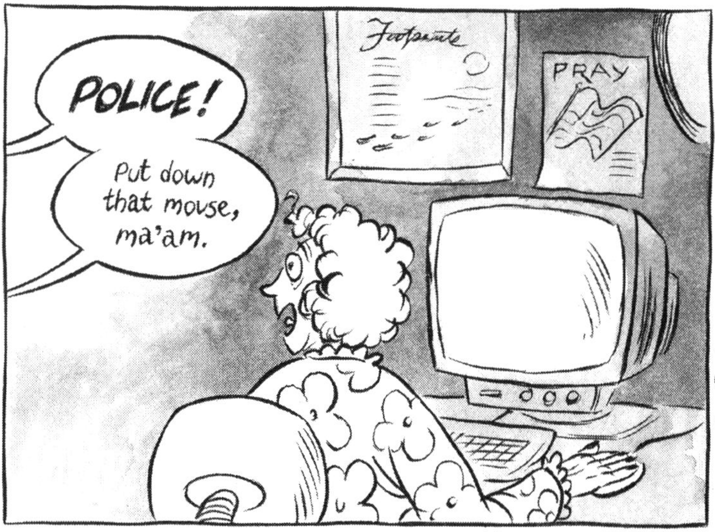
POLICE!
Put down that mouse, ma'am.
PRAY

*The sad case of Dorothy McNutt of Snellville, Georgia—prosecuted under anti-spamming laws by members of her own ladies' prayer circle.*

How have you sinned, my child?
It's all on my blog, father.
Sam Torode

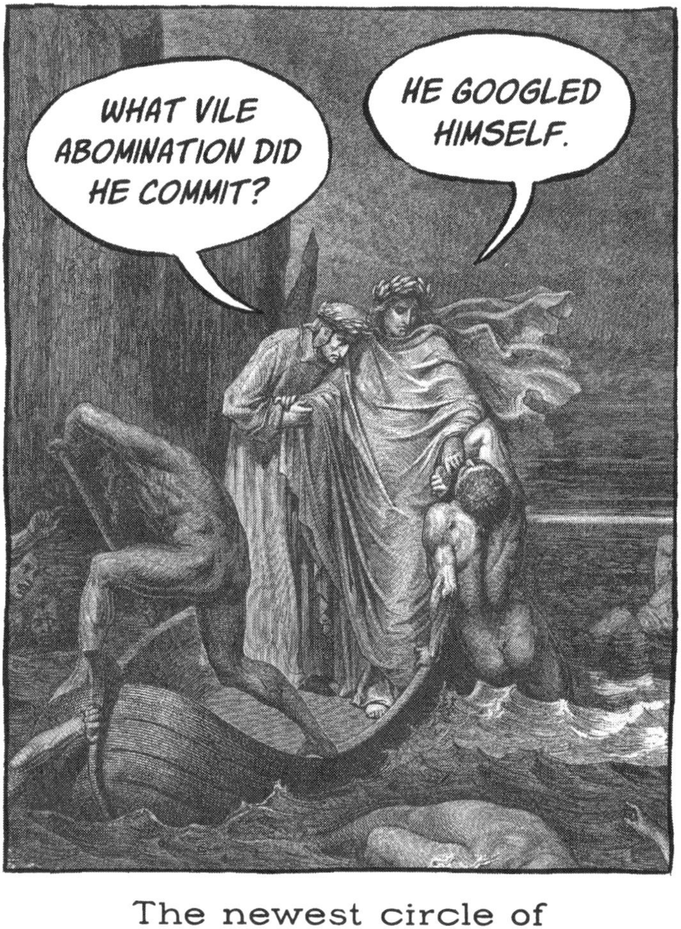
WHAT VILE ABOMINATION DID HE COMMIT?
HE GOOGLED HIMSELF.

The newest circle of
Dante's inferno

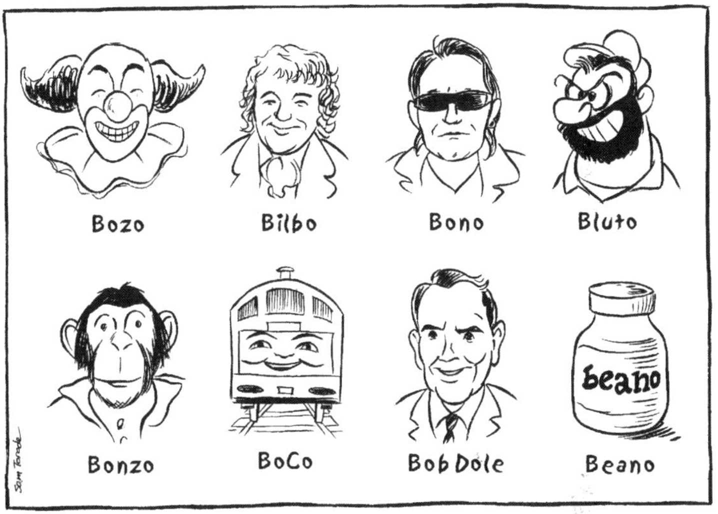
Bozo
Bilbo
Bono
Bluto
Bonzo
BoCo
Bob Dole
beano
Beano
Sam Torode

Which one do you feel like today?

finis.